MONSTER MATH

WORKBOOK

BOOK ONE

Ages 6 to 8

By Mary Cron and Martha Cheney

Illustrated by Yvonne Cherbak

 Lowell House

Juvenile

Los Angeles

CONTEMPORARY BOOKS

Chicago

Reviewed and endorsed by Arthur Benjamin, Ph.D., professor of mathematics at Harvey Mudd College, Claremont, California, and author of *Teach Your Child Math* and *Mathemagics*

Lowell House Books can be purchased at special discounts when ordered in bulk for premiums and special sales. Contact Department JH at the following address:

Lowell House Juvenile
2029 Century Park East, Suite 3290
Los Angeles, CA 90067

Manufactured in the United States of America

ISBN: 1-56565-307-6

10 9 8 7 6 5 4

Note to Parents

Monster Math is a wonderful learning tool that will give your child a head start in math. Not only is there a team of creative monster instructors to present the activities, but the cognitive and deductive skills learned will create a solid foundation in analytical thinking that your child can build upon with continued education.

The activities in this book contain a range of difficulty levels, from basic addition and subtraction to beginning multiplication, division, and fractions. It is important that your child complete the activities in order, since the book progresses from simple counting skills to more advanced problem solving. Skipping activities that appear early in the book may cause frustration later.

Let your child work at his or her own pace—four or five pages at a time may be enough for one sitting. After each activity is completed, have your child turn to the back of the book to check the answers. If an answer is incorrect, review the problem (together if necessary), making sure your child understands everything before moving to the next activity.

Written by teachers and endorsed by a professor of mathematics, **Monster Math** will benefit any child who has a desire to learn. Once your child has completed the book, try creating new monster story problems to solve. You may find your child loves learning math—and has the skills to prove it!

SPOOKY MONSTER PARADE

Tonight is the night for the spookiest Halloween parade in town. But the parade can't start until the monsters get in line.

Help the monsters line up in the right order. The first monster is 1. The last monster is 10. They both have moved into line and are standing behind pumpkins. Fill in each pumpkin with the correct number, so the other monsters know where to stand in line.

THE HALLOWEEN PARTY

The monsters are having a good time! They love Halloween parties.

Some monsters have caramel apples.

Some monsters are playing Pin the Tail on the Black Cat.

Some monsters are carrying trick-or-treat bags. These monsters are confused—they should be out in the neighborhood trick-or-treating!

How many monsters have caramel apples? _____

How many monsters are playing Pin the Tail? _____

Draw a ◯ around every monster who should be out trick-or-treating.

How many monsters are at the party? _____

THE DANCE

Monsters love to dance! Everyone is wearing special dancing shoes. But the monsters can't dance until they find their partners who are wearing the same kinds of shoes.

You can help the monsters on the left find their partners on the right. Draw a line to connect the partners who are wearing the same kinds of shoes.

How many sets of partners are at the dance? _____

Put a ◯ around the monster without a partner.

The monsters are having a great time dancing! Mr. Masher, who wears glasses, is looking for his child. His child has:

a pointed hat
a belt
six fingers
a bandaged knee
a watch
an untied shoe
a crooked nose

How many monsters are dancing? _____

How many pairs are dancing? _____

How many monsters wear a belt? _____

How many monsters have a bandaged knee? _____

How many monsters have a crooked nose? _____

Circle Mr. Masher's child.

A MONSTER MONTH

Mikey Monster is making a calendar for the month of May. He wants to make sure that he remembers to celebrate his birthday! Help him fill in the missing numbers on his calendar.

Use these clues to figure out the date of Mikey's birthday.

- It is a number greater than 5.
- It ends with a zero.
- It does not fall on a Saturday.
- It is a number less than 24.

Put a star on the calendar to mark Mikey's birthday.

A MONSTER TENNIS MATCH

All of these monsters have come to the tennis court to play in a tournament. How many are there?

Instead of counting the monsters in the usual way, we can count by 2's. We see that there are 2 monsters in the first pair, so we put a 2 on the line beneath them. 2 more monsters make 4. Now fill in the rest of the blanks by yourself! Can you count by 2's up to 20? Up to 100?

GO, TEAM, GO!

The two teams have just arrived at the playing field. Before they start their game, count the monsters on both pages to make sure everyone is here.

How many players are wearing odd numbers? ____

How many players are wearing even numbers? ____

How many coaches are here? ____

Put a ☐ around the character who is not a part of the team.

Put the monsters into their two teams. The monsters wearing odd numbers are on Team #1. The monsters wearing even numbers are on Team #2. Write their numbers on the team clipboards below. (Don't forget to include the coaches' numbers on the clipboards.)

Team # 1

_____
_____
_____
_____
_____

Team # 2

_____
_____
_____
_____
_____

Now solve the problem below to find out which team wins! If the answer is an odd number, Team #1 wins. If the answer is an even number, Team #2 wins.

$$4 + 2 + 0 = \underline{\quad}$$

Circle all the players who are on the winning team.

THE FEARSOME FRUNDELLS

The Frundell family is a very unusual monster family. They are known as the Fearsome Frundells because each member of the family has 5 frightening horns growing out of his or her head. How many horns do the Fearsome Frundells have all together?

We don't have to count the horns one by one to find out! We can count by 5's.

 5   10   ____   ____   ____

We know that each monster has 5 horns, so we can begin with the number 5. 5 plus 5 more is 10, so we can put a 10 on the next line. 10 and 5 more equal what number? Write it under the third monster. Finish the rest of the row by yourself!

TOO MANY FLIES

One hot summer day Thor decided to take a nap in the shade. He couldn't get to sleep because of all the flies buzzing around his head. He tried to count them, but that made him dizzy! See if you can estimate how many flies are bothering Thor just by looking. Don't count them yet. Write your estimate on this line. _____

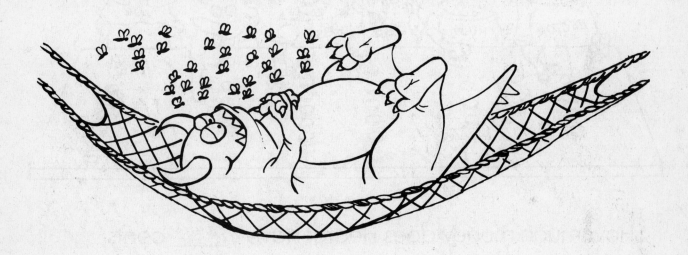

Now, to check your estimate, count the flies in groups of 10. Draw a circle around each group of 10.

How many groups of 10 flies are there? _____
How many flies are left over? _____
How many flies are there altogether? _____

SPENDING MONEY

Hector and Hugh, Gerta and Gussie, and Mug and Lug are getting ready to go to the store. They are counting their pennies. Each penny is worth 1 cent.

How much money does Hector have? _____ cents

How much money does Hugh have? _____ cents

How much do Hector and Hugh have? _____ cents

How much do Gerta and Gussie have? _____ cents

How much do Mug and Lug have? _____ cents

Put an **X** on the pair who have the most money.

Circle the pair who have the least amount of money.

MONSTER SHOPPING

The monsters have counted their money. They are going to buy things at the store. Look at each item on sale. Then answer each question by putting an **X** by the pair who has enough money to buy the object.

Who can buy the toothbrush? ____ Hector and Hugh
____ Gerta and Gussie
____ Mug and Lug

Who can buy the grapes? ____ Hector and Hugh
____ Gerta and Gussie
____ Mug and Lug

Who can buy the apple? ____ Hector and Hugh
____ Gerta and Gussie
____ Mug and Lug

Who can buy the doll? ____ Hector and Hugh
____ Gerta and Gussie
____ Mug and Lug

What would you buy? _____

How much money would you need? ____ cents

PLANTING A GARDEN

The monsters are planting a vegetable garden. They're going to do all the work themselves! Their favorite vegetables are carrots, peas, and beans. They taste great with worms in monster stew!

How many monsters have a 🔨? ____

How many monsters have a ____? ____

How many tools do you see? ____

Joot has 2 packets of carrot seeds.
Moot has 3 packets of pea seeds.
Hoot has 1 packet of bean seeds.

Find out how many seed packets the monsters have by adding up the numbers below. Then fill in the blank.

2 + 3 + 1= ____

16

Here's a chart that shows the number of plants each monster is growing. Add up how many of each kind of vegetable they have planted. Fill in the totals at the bottom of the chart, then answer the questions below.

VEGETABLES →	🥕	🫛	🫘
JOOT	5	1	2
MOOT	1	6	1
HOOT	2	1	4
TOTAL			

How many carrots are the monsters growing? ____

How many peas are the monsters growing? ____

How many beans are the monsters growing? ____

How many plants are growing altogether? ____

SWEET THINGS

The monsters love to bake sweet things. Their favorites are snail tarts, slime cookies, and thorny cream puffs. Simon and Stella are planning what they are each going to bake.

Fill in the blanks below to find out how many sweet things Simon will bake:

3 + 2 = _____

6 + 3 = _____

4 + 3 = _____

TOTAL _____

Fill in the blanks below to find out how many sweet things Stella will bake:

3 + 4 = _____

3 + 6 = _____

2 + 5 = _____

TOTAL _____

Circle who will bake the most sweets.

18

TROUBLE IN THE BAKERY!

While Simon and Stella were in the back washing dishes, Simon's twin nephews came to visit. The nephews gobbled down some treats. They knocked over some bowls. They even sat on some pastries!

Simon made a list of all the sweets he and Stella lost. Can you help him add up the ruined sweets, then put the totals in the boxes below?

SWEETS →					
(Stella)	6	4	9	5	7
(Simon)	3	3	1	2	2
TOTAL					

Which sweet did the twins eat or destroy the most?

READING THE MUSIC

Delbert's first day of band practice is tomorrow. He is trying to read his music. How many different kinds of notes do you see? Count them and then add them up below.

___ + ___ + ___ + ___ = ___

Put a ◯ around the kind of note(s) that is used the most.

Put an **X** on the kind of note(s) that is used the least.

20

MONSTERS IN THE BAND

The monsters are waiting for their band instruments to arrive. There are tubas, flutes, trumpets, and bells. Can you figure out how many monsters play each of the instruments? Use the clues below to answer each question.

More than 5 but less than 7 monsters play the trumpet.
   How many play the trumpet? _____
Less than 4 but more than 2 monsters play the flute.
   How many play the flute? _____
More than 1 but less than 3 monsters play the tuba.
   How many play the tuba? _____
More than 3 but less than 5 monsters play the bells.
   How many play the bells? _____

Circle the instrument that is played the most.

Put an **X** over the instrument that is played the least.

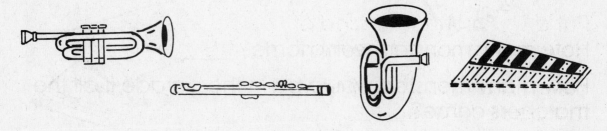

IT'S A PARADE!

The monster parade is about to begin. But only 6 monsters are ready to march! There were more marchers, but some had to go home. Read what happened to the missing marchers, then answer the questions at the bottom of the page.

1 broke her toe.

2 lost their music.

1 caught a cold.

2 were too big to fit into their uniforms.

How many monsters went home? _____

How many monsters would be in the parade if all the marchers came? _____

WATCHING THE PARADE!

Monsters love parades! There are so many monsters, nobody can see what they look like—except for Fred. Fred took his binoculars up in a tree to see how many monsters were at the parade.

Add or subtract the numbers to find out what Fred counted:

2 + 3 + 1 = _____ have chalk on their noses.

6 + 2 – 2 = _____ have pencils behind their ears.

5 – 1 – 2 = _____ have holes in their socks.

4 – 1 – 1 = _____ have dinosaur backpacks.

4 + 3 + 2 = _____ have skinned knees.

Add the totals above to find out how many monsters Fred spotted altogether. _____

MONSTER CAFE

What a feast! Eight monsters are eating a delicious dinner at the Monster Cafe. The chef has cooked his favorite meal of snails, worms, and dirt sandwiches!

Everything was going fine, until. . .

Twister left to answer the telephone.
Toot went home because she forgot her money.
Buster left to pick up his sister at the bus stop.

How many monsters had to leave the table? _____

After Twister, Toot, and Buster left, how many chairs were empty? _____

How many monsters were left at the table? _____

A BUSY MONSTER COOK!

Moot, the cook at the Monster Cafe, is working very hard. He has many orders to fill. Look on the Menu to see what the most popular dishes are.

Count all the orders below. How many orders does Moot have to fill? ____

menu

Snail Soup

Worm Pasta

Dirt Sandwich

Moot worked very fast and filled:

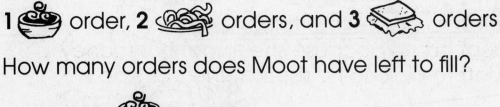

1 order, **2** orders, and **3** orders

How many orders does Moot have left to fill?

____ more order(s)

____ more order(s)

____ more order(s)

MILES AND HIS MARBLES

Once there was a very silly monster named Miles, who spent every day playing marbles. He kept his 20 favorite marbles in a beautiful marble bag. One day he grabbed his marbles and went to play with his friends.

At Wilbur's house he lost 10 marbles. How many marbles did he have left? Fill in the blank and carry down the total to the next blank.

$$20 - 10 = \underline{\hspace{1cm}}$$

At Rosie's house he lost 2 more! Carry down the total to the next blank.

$$\underline{\hspace{1cm}} - 2 = \underline{\hspace{1cm}}$$

At Fuddy's house he lost 3 more! $\underline{\hspace{1cm}} - 3 = \underline{\hspace{1cm}}$

At Matilda's house he lost 4 more! $\underline{\hspace{1cm}} - 4 = \underline{\hspace{1cm}}$

What a sad day for Miles! How many marbles did he have left? $\underline{\hspace{1cm}}$

Wilbur put the marbles he won from Miles into a bag. 5 of the marbles are white and 5 of them are black. Wilbur wants to give his brother Warren 2 of the marbles, but Warren wants the marbles to be the same color. If Wilbur reaches into his bag **without looking**, how many marbles will he have to pull out to make sure that he gets 2 of the same color?

Let's say the first marble Wilbur pulls out of the bag is black. Next he pulls out a white marble. The third marble is sure to match one of the first 2.

Why?_____

Is it possible that Wilbur could pull out matching marbles in 2 tries?_____
_____

MENTAL MONSTER MATH

Try to figure out the following problem as you read it. Do the adding and subtracting in your head. Use a pencil and paper only if you get stuck!

Mary and Marvin asked all their friends to come to the park to play baseball. Mary, Marvin, and 10 other monsters arrived at the park at 10 o'clock. 3 more monsters arrived at 11:00. At 12:00, 4 monsters had to go home for lunch, and 1 had to leave for a dentist appointment. At 1:00 the McGuire twins arrived, along with Marvin's cousin Milton.

How many monsters were at the park at 11:00?_____

How many monsters were at the park at 12:00?_____

How many monsters were at the park at 1:00?_____

MIBBY PLAYS CARDS

Mibby the monster always wins every card game she plays! It's the start of a new game. Look at all the cards in her hand.

How many cards does she have? ___

Before the game is over, she has to give:

3 black cat cards to May
2 snake cards to Jud
3 bat cards to Wooster
1 frog card to Mitsy

How many cards does Mibby have left? ___

Mibby needs to have more than 6 cards to win the game.

Does she win?

YES   NO

THE MONSTERS RECYCLE

The monsters want to take better care of the earth, so they have started their own recycling center! Right now Dit, Dat, and Dot are collecting cans, bottles, and newspapers, and separating them into different recycling bins.

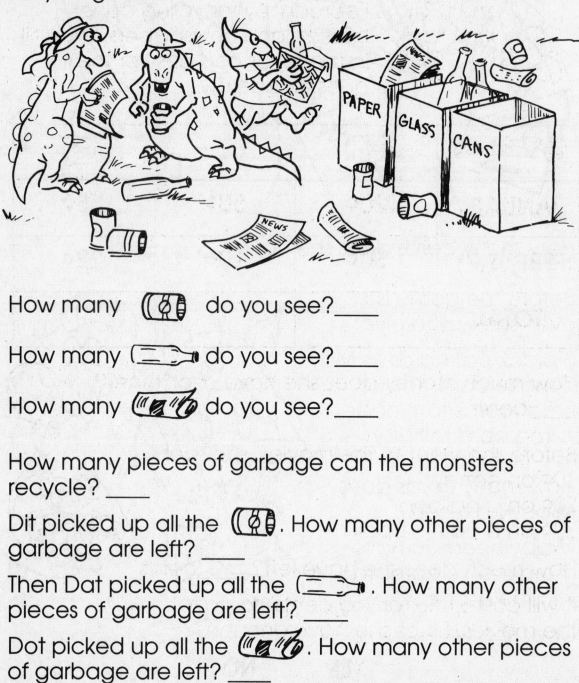

How many do you see?____

How many do you see?____

How many do you see?____

How many pieces of garbage can the monsters recycle? ____

Dit picked up all the . How many other pieces of garbage are left? ____

Then Dat picked up all the . How many other pieces of garbage are left? ____

Dot picked up all the . How many other pieces of garbage are left? ____

TURN GARBAGE INTO MONEY

Dot has learned that she can earn money by recycling. She is saving her money so she can go to the movies. Count the money she earned in January and February by recycling cans, bottles, and newspapers. Then fill in the totals and answer the questions below.

GARBAGE →			
JANUARY	20¢	50¢	35¢
FEBRUARY	50¢	10¢	22¢
TOTAL			

How much money does she have altogether?
____ cents

Before she went to the movies, she spent:
10¢ on candy
20¢ on a balloon
30¢ on a comic book

How much does she have left? ____ cents

It will cost $1.50 (or 150 cents) to go to the movies. Does she have enough?

YES   **NO**

SECRET NUMBERS

Rosie is trying to open the safe. But she doesn't know the numbers that will open the lock. She doesn't know what's inside the safe either! Rosie hopes it's gold! You can help her.

Fill in the answers to the mystery math problems, then put an **X** in the EVEN column if the answer is even, or in the ODD column if it's odd.

NUMBER	EVEN	ODD
7 + 3 + 4 = _____		
8 − 5 + 3 = _____		
2 + 2 + 3 = _____		
9 − 3 + 2 = _____		
6 + 2 − 2 = _____		

If there are more than 2 odd numbers and less than 4 even numbers, then frogs are in the safe.

If there are more than 3 even numbers and less than 2 odd numbers, then gold is in the safe.

Put a ◯ around the treasure that Rosie found in the safe.

MONSTER SOUP

Once upon a time, 2 very hungry monsters named Zort and Zerta went looking for tasty things to put in their soup. Zort found 5 snails asleep under a bush.

"Mmm, delicious!" he said. He put the snails into his pockets.

Zerta found 3 rotten apples in the dirt by a fence.

"Terrific!" she snorted, stuffing the apples into her basket.

They headed home to their kitchen, but on the way, 1 tricky snail slowly crawled out of Zort's pocket and escaped.

How many things can the monsters put in <u>their soup</u>?

_____ 🐌 + _____ 🍎 = _____ 🍎 − _____ 🐌 = _____ 🍎
🐌

BREAK THE SECRET CODE!

The monsters love to break secret codes. They also love movies! In fact, they think they know everything about every movie ever made. But they're not as smart as they think!

They have to discover the name of a famous movie song, and you can help them by breaking the secret code below. In the code, every letter stands for a number. Solve the problems on the next page to find out which letter goes in each blank. If all your answers are correct, you'll soon discover the mystery song title!

SECRET CODE KEY

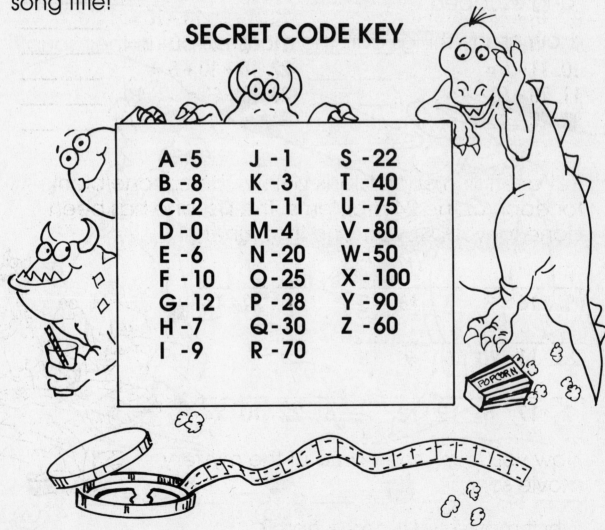

A - 5	J - 1	S - 22
B - 8	K - 3	T - 40
C - 2	L - 11	U - 75
D - 0	M - 4	V - 80
E - 6	N - 20	W - 50
F - 10	O - 25	X - 100
G - 12	P - 28	Y - 90
H - 7	Q - 30	Z - 60
I - 9	R - 70	

Here are 24 problems. Solve each of them and write
down the sums. Then, find the letter in the secret
code key that corresponds to each sum. The first one
has been done for you.

Number / Letter   Number / Letter

1. $5 + 5 + 5 - 5 =$ 10   F   13. $20 + 20 + 10 =$ ___ ___
2. $6 + 6 - 4 =$ ___ ___   14. $18 - 6 - 6 =$ ___ ___
3. $3 + 2 + 10 - 4 =$ ___ ___   15. $70 + 30 - 50 =$ ___ ___
4. $70 - 30 =$ ___ ___   16. $10 + 5 + 10 =$ ___ ___
5. $20 + 30 - 41 =$ ___ ___   17. $20 + 20 + 30 =$ ___ ___
6. $3 + 2 + 6 =$ ___ ___   18. $20 + 10 - 5 =$ ___ ___
7. $3 + 3 + 6 - 1 =$ ___ ___   19. $18 + 4 - 20 =$ ___ ___
8. $15 + 15 + 40 =$ ___ ___   20. $6 + 5 + 10 - 10 =$ ___ ___
9. $10 + 5 + 10 =$ ___ ___   21. $12 + 8 - 10 - 3 =$ ___ ___
10. $11 - 6 =$ ___ ___   22. $10 + 10 + 5 =$ ___ ___
11. $70 - 60 - 4 =$ ___ ___   23. $40 + 50 =$ ___ ___
12. $20 + 4 - 21 =$ ___ ___   24. $16 + 4 + 50 - 70 =$ ___ ___

Put a letter in each blank below. There is one blank
for each of the 24 problems. The first one has been
done for you. Now, name that tune!

 F ___ ___ ___ ___ ___   ___ ___ ___
 1   16   3   7 18 13   4   21 14

___ ___ ___ ___ ___ ___
23 11 20   6   9 15

___ ___ ___ ___ ___   ___ ___ ___ ___
 2 17   5 19 12   8 22 10 24

Now you know the name of the mystery
movie song!

What movie did it come from? _____

THE KEYS ARE MISSING!

Vinnie and Vivian are brother and sister. They have lost their house keys. They have to be home at 6 o'clock to cook dinner for their family. They know they left the keys at a place they visited today. They've been to the Monster Cafe, the Witch's House, the Elf Cave, and the Troll Tree House. Use the clues in the box below and the map on the next page to help them get to the place where they left their keys.

CLUE BOX

1. Go to the number that is less than 20 and made with two 1's.

2. Then subtract 4 from that number, and add 7.

3. Next add 2 six times to that number.

4. Then go to the number that is a reversal of the number you are on.

5. Following that, subtract 10 six times from that number.

6. Next add 7 to that number, and subtract 8.

7. After that add 20 to that number.

8. Then subtract 6 three times from that number.

9. Finally, add 7 to that number, then add a 0 to the end.

Put a marker in the START square. Solve each problem in the clue box, and move your marker to the number box that matches each answer. You may go in any direction.

If you answer all the clues correctly, you will land on the place where Vinnie and Vivian left their keys.

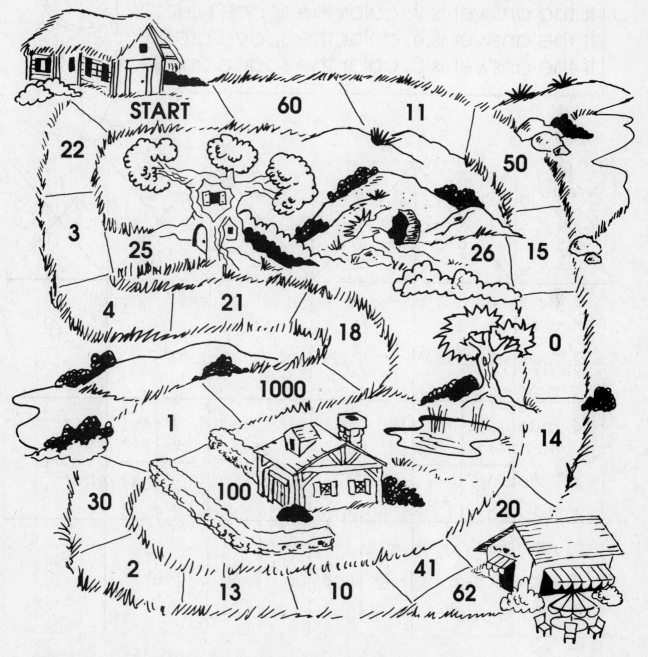

Where did the monsters leave their keys? _____

COLOR BY NUMBER

Help the monster complete the problems in the grid below. Color them according to the chart.

If the answer is 3, color the space blue.
If the answer is 4, color the space green.
If the answer is 5, color the space purple.

Row 1 (triangular cells):

19 − 8 | 13 − 5 | 4 + 4 | 9 + 2 | 11 − 5 | 9 + 1
4 + 9 | 19 − 3 | 16 + 1 | 5 + 2 | 10 + 6 | 11 − 2 | 10 + 10 | 7 + 7 | 6 + 6 | 12 + 2 | 8 + 8 | 5 + 5
15 − 12 | 8 − 5 | 16 − 3 | 12 + 1 | 13 − 10 | 11 − 8

Row 2:

3 + 1 | 9 − 5 | 12 + 9 | 14 + 3 | 23 − 19 | 20 − 16

Row 3:

2 + 2 | 8 − 4 | 11 − 6 | 16 − 12 | 25 − 21 | 3 + 2 | 7 − 2 | 15 − 11
| 13 − 9 | 1 + 3 | | | 12 − 8 | 17 − 13 |

Row 4:

5 − 1 | 6 − 2 | 19 − 15 | 13 − 8 | 16 − 11 | 14 − 10 | 18 − 14 | 14 − 10

38

MONSTER MAZES

Begin at the sign that says START. Move from a number to a plus or minus sign, then to another number as shown. You can only move to a square that touches the square you are in. Find a path that leads to the answer, which is marked EXIT.

One Monster Maze has been done for you. Help the monsters solve the other one!

START

2	+	3	
+	1	-	4
3	-		+
-	2	=	3

2
EXIT

START

4	-	2	+
-	1	+	3
4	+	2	-
3	-	=	1

4
EXIT

39

OUT TO LUNCH!

These monsters want to go to the pizza parlor. But they can't go until they know how much money they have to spend. You can help them! Count how much money each monster has, then fill in the blanks below.

How much money does Bob have? ＿＿ cents

How much money does Babs have? ＿＿ cents

How much money does Dot have? ＿＿ cents

How much do they have altogether? ＿＿ cents

The monsters are waiting to order. Look on the previous page to find out how much money they have, then answer the question below.

MENU

All-You-Can-Eat Pizza $2.50 (250¢)
Soup $1.25 per bowl (125¢)
Lemonade $.25 per glass (25¢)

What can each of the monsters buy with the money they have? _____

IN THE GYM!

The monsters are getting in shape. Some think they are too fat. Some think they are too thin. Some want to get stronger. Look at the different ways they are working out, then go to the next page.

Answer the question, then fill in the blanks below. The first one has been done for you.

How many monsters are exercising at the gym? ____

__1__ out of 10 monsters, or $\frac{1}{10}$ of the monsters, are touching their toes.

____ out of 10 monsters, or ____/10 of the monsters, are hanging upside down.

____ out of 10 monsters, or ____/10 of the monsters, are riding bikes.

____ out of 10 monsters, or ____/10 of the monsters, are running on the treadmill.

____ out of 10 monsters, or ____/10 of the monsters, are lifting weights.

____ out of 10 monsters, or ____/10 of the monsters, are doing leg lifts.

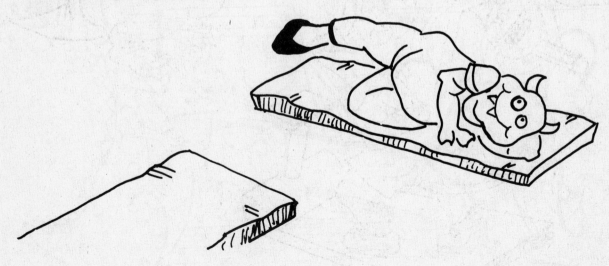

MONSTER RECESS

It is recess time at Slimepit Elementary School, and all the little monsters have gone out to play. Mrs. Murky is watching the playground to find out what activities the monsters like best. She is making a graph so that she can show the other teachers what she has learned. Can you help her complete the graph?

Fill in one box for each child.

ball					
jump rope					
sandbox					
jungle gym					

Do more children like the jungle gym or the sandbox? Which activity is the most popular?

MONSTER MOON

The monsters are studying the moon. It changes its appearance as the month goes by. Sometimes you can see the full moon in the night sky. Sometimes you can see only part of it. When only part of the moon is showing, it is a fraction of its full size.

Help the monsters learn fractions by filling in the blanks below.

Pretend the moon is divided into 2 equal parts.

$2/2$ The moon is full. The monsters see both of its 2 parts.

$1/2$ This is a half moon. The monsters see only ____ of its 2 parts.

What if you divided the moon into 4 equal parts?

$4/4$ The moon is full. The monsters can see all 4 of its ____ parts.

$3/4$ The moon is almost full. The monsters can see ____ of the 4 parts.

——$/4$ The moon is half full. The monsters can see ____ of the 4 parts.

——$/4$ The moon is almost gone. Only ____ part is left.

UP IN SPACE!

The monsters are on their way to the farthest part of the galaxy. Answer the questions below.

How many objects do they see out the window? ____

How many  do they see? ____

How many do they see? ____

How many do they see? ____

How many do they see? ____

Look at the picture above, then fill in the blanks below.

——/8 of the objects are ⟨rocket⟩ .

——/8 of the objects are ⟨comet⟩ .

——/8 of the objects are ⟨planet⟩ .

——/8 of the objects are ⟨star⟩ .

SAVING MONSTER MONEY

The monsters are saving their money to go to the amusement park next week. They are doing all the chores they can! Every chore brings in money.

Look at the chart to see how much money they earn each day for each chore they finish. Then answer the questions below to find out how much money the monsters will have to take to the amusement park.

They swept floors on 3 different days. How much did they earn? ____ cents

The monsters dusted on 4 different days. How much did they earn? ____ cents

They mopped the floors on the same days they swept the floors. How much did they earn for mopping? ____ cents

They washed dishes on 6 different days. How much did they earn? ____ cents

How much money did the monsters earn for the whole week? ____ cents

CHORES	MONEY
(broom)	10¢
(duster)	20¢
(mop)	40¢
(dishes)	50¢

AT THE AMUSEMENT PARK!

The monsters, with their money in their pockets, ran all the way to the amusement park. They want to buy tickets to go on the rides.

Ferris wheel   20¢
Merry-go-round   10¢
Pony ride   50¢
Bumper car   15¢

Look on the previous page to find out how much they earned: ____ cents or $ ____

How much money would they spend on each ride if all 3 monsters go on every ride once?

Fill in the blanks below.

Ferris wheel tickets   ____ cents
Merry-go-round tickets   ____ cents
Pony ride tickets   ____ cents
Bumper car tickets   ____ cents

How much money do they have left over? ____ cents

Which rides would you want to go on? _____

MONSTER PIZZA

While the monsters were at the amusement park, they all got hungry. They went to the pizza stand for a snack.

Mug ate 1/2 of a pizza.
Lug ate 2/4 of a pizza.
Gug ate 3/6 of a pizza.

Color in the portion of pizza that each monster ate.

Which monster ate the most pizza? _____

Explain your answer. _____
_____
_____
_____

TROLL MOUNTAIN SECRET

The trolls came during the night. They left a secret number combination in the square rocks. Solve the math problems below to help the monsters unlock the door to Troll Mountain. There's gold inside! (Hint: It will help you to count the boxes in each problem.)

4 x 2 = ____

4 x 3 = ____

3 x ____ = ____

4 x ____ = ____

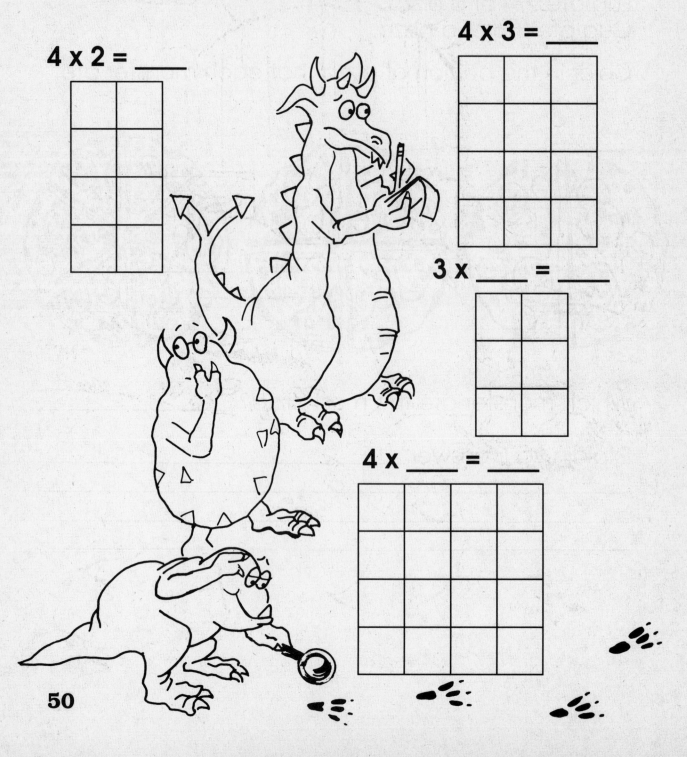

50

Add up the 4 final answers to the problems the trolls left on the previous page to open the mountain door. If the total of the 4 answers is correct (the answer is on page 63), the door will unlock, and the troll's gold will be in the monster's paws. Write the answer on the combination lock below.

BUGS IN THE CLOSET!

Datto is very busy! He can't find his hat. He couldn't find his red shoe. So he decided it was time to clean his closet.

But after he got to work, Datto found more than clothes in his closet! He found little monster bugs everywhere! Fill in the blanks below to help him find out how many bugs are in his closet.

Datto has 4 ties and on every tie there are 2 bugs. ____ bugs are on his ties.

Datto has 3 sweaters and on every sweater there is 1 bug. ____ bugs are on his sweaters.

Datto has 2 hats and on every hat there are 5 bugs. ____ bugs are on his hats.

Datto has 6 shirts and on every shirt there are 2 bugs. ____ bugs are on his shirts.

How many monster bugs did Datto find altogether in his closet? ____

SHOES AND SOCKS

Mit has 4 kinds of shoes and 3 kinds of socks. She has made this chart to help her see what the socks and shoes will look like together.

How many different sock-and-shoe combinations can she make? _____

(Hint: It will help to draw each sock-and-shoe combination in the squares provided.)

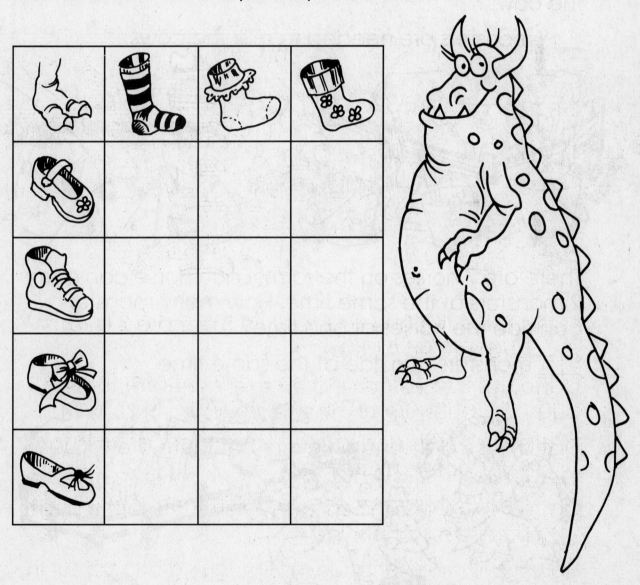

MONSTERS AT THE FARM

The monsters are having a wonderful time at the farm! Everybody has a special job to do. Some milk cows, and others ride horses. Solve the problems below to find out how many monsters are needed for each job.

There are 4 cows to be milked. Each cow needs 3 monsters to milk it. How many monsters get to milk the cows?

____ monsters are needed to milk the cows.

There are 7 horses on the farm. Each horse can carry 2 monsters at the same time. How many monsters can ride the horses at one time?

____ monsters can ride at the same time.

This monster farmer is going to pick some apples off his trees. He has 3 trees. If he picks 2 apples off each tree, how many apples will he have in his basket?

Draw the apples in the basket. Below it, write a number sentence that explains your answer.

| _____ | X | _____ | = | _____ |
| apples from each tree | | trees | | total apples |

PROBLEMS ON THE FARM

Read each problem. Then write a number sentence and draw the apples in the basket to show your answer.

If the farmer picks 1 apple off each tree, how many apples will he have?

_____ x _____ = _____

If the farmer picks 3 apples off each tree, how many apples will he have?

_____ x _____ = _____

If the farmer picks 4 apples off each tree, how many apples will he have?

_____ x _____ = _____

A DAY FOR A PICNIC

These 6 monsters are hungry! Their picnic lunch is ready! Look at the picture and count up each of the food items. Then divide the food equally to find out what each monster will eat. Put the answers in the blanks.

____ lollipops

____ cupcakes

____ apples

____ carrots

____ drinks

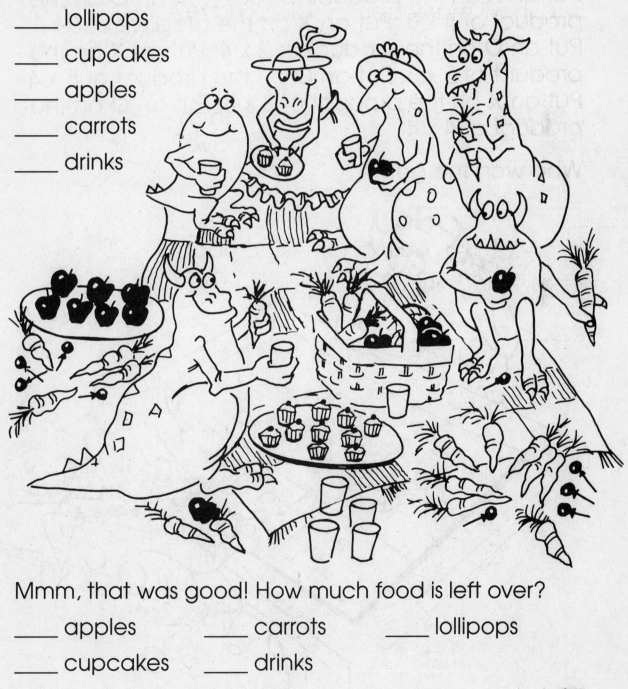

Mmm, that was good! How much food is left over?

____ apples ____ carrots ____ lollipops

____ cupcakes ____ drinks

FIND THE WINNING MONSTER

Bugsy and Bonnie are playing tic-tac-toe. Bugsy is **X** and Bonnie is **O**. Solve these problems to see who wins! Remember that a **product** is the answer to a multiplication problem.

Put an **X** on the product of 3 x 2. Put an **O** on the product of 4 x 3. Put an **X** on the product of 5 x 1. Put an **O** on the product of 2 x 4. Put an **X** on the product of 5 x 3. Put an **O** on the product of 5 x 4. Put an **X** on the product of 3 x 3. Put an **O** on the product of 4 x 4.

Who won the game?

MONSTER LOGIC

Maggie, Fred, and Gus went to a birthday party. They each brought flowers and a gift. Use the clues to find out in what order they arrived at the party and what they each brought. Fill in the chart.

Maggie did not arrive last.
The monster who brought mugwort arrived first.
The monster who brought dandelions arrived before the monster who brought some stinky cheese.
The monster who brought a mousetrap did not arrive first or last.
Maggie brought a flyswatter.
Gus arrived after Fred.

arrived	first	second	third
monster			
flowers			
gift			

ANSWERS

page 4
2, 3, 4, 5, 6, 7, 8, 9

page 5
2, 3, 8

page 6
3

page 7
7, 3, 4, 3, 1

page 8

page 9
2, 4, 6, 8, 10

page 10
5, 5, 2

page 11
Team #1: 1, 5, 9, 11, 17
Team #2: 2, 4, 10, 16, 20
6

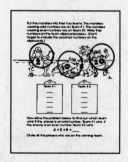

page 12

5, 10, 15, 20, 25

page 13

3, 0, 30

page 14

4, 4, 8, 12, 18

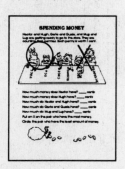

page 15

Mug and Lug can buy the
   toothbrush.
All three pairs can buy the grapes.
Gerta and Gussie, and Mug and Lug
   can buy the apple.
None of them can buy the doll.

page 16

2, 1, 4, 6

page 17

8, 8, 7
8, 8, 7, 23

page 18

5, 9, 7, 21
7, 9, 7, 23
Stella will bake the most sweets.

page 19

9, 7, 10, 7, 9
The twins destroyed the most
slime cookies.

page 20

2, 3, 3, 1, 9

page 21

6, 3, 2, 4
The trumpet is played the most.
The tuba is played the least.

page 22

6, 12

page 23

6, 6, 2, 2, 9, 25

page 24

3, 3, 5

page 25

9
2, 0, 1

page 26

10, 10, 8, 8, 5, 5, 1, 1

page 27

The third marble is sure to match one of
the first 2 because there are only 2 kinds
of marbles! Yes, a matching pair could
be pulled out in 2 tries.

page 28

15, 10, 13

61

page 29
16, 7, YES

page 30
6, 4, 5, 15, 9, 5, 0

page 31
70¢, 60¢, 57¢
187, 127
NO

page 32
14, Even
6, Even
7, Odd
8, Even
6, Even
Rosie found gold in the safe.

page 33
5, 3, 8, 1, 7

page 35
(1) 10-F, (2) 8-B, (3) 11-L, (4) 40-T,
(5) 9-I, (6) 11-L, (7) 11-L, (8) 70-R,
(9) 25-O, (10) 5-A, (11) 6-E, (12) 3-K,
(13) 50-W, (14) 6-E, (15) 50-W, (16) 25-O,
(17) 70-R, (18) 25-O, (19) 2-C, (20) 11-L,
(21) 7-H, (22) 25-O, (23) 90-Y, (24) 0-D
FOLLOW THE YELLOW BRICK ROAD
The Wizard of Oz

page 37
(1) 11, (2) 14, (3) 26, (4) 62, (5) 2, (6) 1,
(7) 21, (8) 3, (9) 100
The Witch's House (100)

page 38
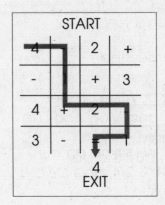

page 39
There is more than one right answer.
Here is one possibility.

page 40
25, 25, 25, 75

page 41
They can each buy one glass of lemonade.

page 43
10
3, 3/10
2, 2/10
1, 1/10
2, 2/10
1, 1/10

page 44

More children like the jungle gym than the sandbox. Jumping rope is the most popular activity.

ball						
jump rope						
sandbox						
jungle gym						

page 45

1, 4, 3, 2/4, 2, 1/4, 1

page 46

8, 2, 2, 2, 2

2/8, 2/8, 2/8, 2/8

page 47

30, 80, 120, 300, 530

page 48

530, $5.30

60, 30, 150, 45, 245

page 49

Each monster ate the same amount of pizza, because 1/2, 2/4, and 3/6 are equivalent fractions!

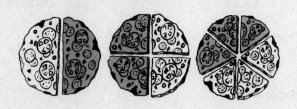

page 50

4 x 2 = 8, 4 x 3 = 12, 3 x 2 = 6, 4 x 4 = 16

page 51

The secret number combination is 42.

page 52

8, 3, 10, 12, 33

page 53

12

page 54

12, 14

page 55

2 x 3 = 6

page 56

1 x 4 = 4

3 x 4 = 12

4 x 4 = 16

page 57

picnic food: 1 lollipop, 2 cupcakes, 2 apples, 3 carrots, 1 drink

leftovers: 1 apple, 0 cupcakes, 2 carrots, 2 drinks, 3 lollipops

page 58

Bugsy won the game.

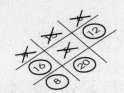

page 59

arrived	first	second	third
monster	Maggie	Fred	Gus
flowers	mugwort	dandelions	thistles
gift	flyswatter	mousetrap	cheese